K-9 POLICE DOGS

BY CARI MEISTER

What are you

curious about?

Curious About is published by
Amicus Learning, an imprint of Amicus
P.O. Box 227, Mankato, MN 56002
www.amicuspublishing.us

Editor: Ana Brauer
Series Designer: Kathleen Petelinsek
Book Designer and Photo Researcher: Sara Hood

Cataloging-in-Publication data is available
from the Library of Congress.
Library Binding ISBN: 9798892008556
Paperback ISBN: 9798892009218
eBook ISBN: 9798892009874
LCCN: 2025012837

Photo Credits: Alamy Stock Photo/Nancy G Fire Photography,
Nancy Greifenhagen, cover, 1, Operation 2022, 8–9;
Dreamstime/Arisha Singh, 3, 17; Getty Images/Agency
Animal Picture, 7 (second from top), alvarez, 7 (top), Fuse, 2,
6, Jordi Janau, 2, 11, Lorado, 10, NurPhoto, 12–13, O2O
Creative, 19, Photographer and Illustrator, 15, Tempura, 21,
TPG, 14; Shutterstock/a katz, 5, Elayne Massaini, 7 (middle),
GoodFocused, 7 (second from bottom), TrapezaStudio,
7 (bottom); The Noun Project/Christine Chapman, 22,
metami septiana, 18, Pong Pong, 22, 23, Rizalwale, 23

Every effort has been made to contact copyright holders for
material reproduced in this book. Any omissions will be rectified
in subsequent printings if notice is given to the publisher.

CHAPTER ONE

What do police dogs do?

Many things! They find people. They **patrol** the streets. They chase down **suspects**. They guard important places. Police dogs also protect their human partners. These dogs are often called K-9s. This is short for "**canine**."

K-9 police dogs work with officers to keep people safe.

What kinds of dogs become police dogs?

A bloodhound can follow a smell for many miles (kilometers).

Police dogs need to be brave and smart! German Shepherds and Rottweilers make good police dogs. They love to learn and work hard. They are also strong and quick. Bloodhounds have a great sense of smell. They help police track things down.

German Shepherd

Belgian Malinois

Rottweiler

Bloodhound

Labrador Retriever

How fast are police dogs?

Very fast! They can run up to 30 miles (48.3 km) per hour! That's faster than any person. Police dogs are strong and **agile**, too. They can jump over walls and climb stairs. They can also crawl quickly and quietly into dangerous places.

When do police dogs start training?

After their first birthday. Before that, their brains and bodies are not ready. They need to wait until they are bigger and stronger. Then, they go to the K-9 police academy with their **handlers**.

Police dogs learn new tricks by playing games with their handlers.

How do police dogs learn their jobs?

They start by playing with special toys, like tugging ropes and rubber balls. They also do agility training. In this training, they run, jump, turn, and climb. This helps them move quickly and safely when they are on the job.

Training courses teach police dogs how to move fast and stay focused.

What special skills do police dogs learn?

Some police dogs learn to "find and bite." They catch a person and wait for help.

Dogs are trained to move quietly and secretly. Their handlers give them special hand signals that tell the dogs to run, attack, or stay still. Some dogs learn to find bombs. When they find one, they sit down quietly. This tells their handler that the bomb is nearby.

How do dogs and handlers become partners?

Dogs and handlers are matched by their personalities. Experts can tell what kind of person will work best with what kind of dog. K-9 teams live and work together. They are just like best friends. They learn to trust each other completely.

K-9 teams build trust by training every day.

What do police dogs do every day?

ON THE CLOCK
K-9 dogs work eight-hour days alongside their handlers.

PATROL DUTY
Keep the area safe.

SCENT WORK
Find missing persons and suspects.

CROWD CONTROL
Help manage large events and protests.

DETECTION
Sniff out drugs and bombs.

Police dogs have busy days! Some check buildings to make sure they're safe. Others use their amazing noses to find hidden things. They sniff for drugs or bombs. Others act as guard dogs for people.

What happens when police dogs retire?

They get to live with their handlers forever! After about eight years of working, these brave dogs become pets. They spend their time getting lots of love from their human family.

DID YOU KNOW?

Someone in the community can adopt the dog if its handler cannot.

Retired police dogs enjoy
lots of rest and play.

ASK MORE QUESTIONS

How do police dogs know which scents to follow?

Can my dog learn police dog tricks?

Try a BIG QUESTION: How do police dogs and their handlers learn to trust each other?

SEARCH FOR ANSWERS

Search the library catalog or the Internet.
A librarian, teacher, or parent can help you.

Using Keywords
Find the looking glass.

Keywords are the most important words in your question.

?

If you want to know about:

- which scents police dogs know to follow, type: K-9 SCENT TRACKING TRAINING

- teaching your dog police tricks, type: TEACHING MY DOG POLICE TRICKS

FIND GOOD SOURCES

Here are some good, safe sources you can use in your research.

Your librarian can help you find more.

Books

Police Dog
by B. Keith Davidson, 2022.

Police Dogs
by Cynthia Argentine, 2023.

Internet Sites

AKC: How a Dog's Nose Supports Police Work
https://www.akc.org/expert-advice/news/how-a-dogs-nose-supports-police-work/
This site gives information about how dogs use their sense of smell in police work.

Britannica: Police Dogs
https://www.britannica.com/topic/police/Police-dogs
This site provides information about the history of police dogs and the kinds of work they do.

Every effort has been made to ensure that these websites are appropriate for children. However, because of the nature of the Internet, it is impossible to guarantee that these sites will remain active indefinitely or that their contents will not be altered.

SHARE AND TAKE ACTION

With an adult, visit a police station that has K-9 officers.

Ask if you can watch a police dog demonstration.

Draw a picture of a police dog team and write a thank you note.

Send it to your local police department.

Make a poster about police dog safety tips to share with your class.

Remember to tell others not to pet police dogs.

GLOSSARY

agile Able to move quickly and smoothly.

canine A domestic dog or a related animal, such as a wolf or fox.

handler The police officer who works with and takes care of a police dog.

patrol To guard an area by walking or driving around it regularly.

suspect A person who might have done something wrong.

INDEX

About the Author

Cari Meister has written many books for children about dogs. She recently rescued a Great Dane puppy from an animal shelter. Cari loves learning about how dogs help keep communities safe. She lives in Vail, Colorado, and sees avalanche dogs at work all winter long.